School
Dictionary

Compiled by Dilys Ross
Illustrated by Mike Phillips and Jane Swift

Published by Ladybird Books Ltd
A Penguin Company
Penguin Books Ltd, 80 Strand, London WC2R 0RL, UK
Penguin Books Australia Ltd, Camberwell, Victoria, Australia
Penguin Books (NZ) Ltd, 67 Apollo Drive, Rosedale, North Shore 0632, New Zealand

10 9 8 7 6 5 4 3 2 1

Printed in China

Contents

Using this dictionary

This dictionary will help you to:

- Find out what words mean
- Check how words are spelt
- Find out more about the words you are using

About this dictionary

- Every definition is written in simple language so that children will be able to understand the meanings easily
- Where several definitions might be possible for a word, (including words that can be used as nouns and verbs) those most appropriate to children in the target age group are included in order to avoid confusion
- Pictures are used to make definitions even easier to understand
- At the back of the book are lots of helpful words listed by subject for quick reference
- Some simple grammatical references are included (see key opposite) to give children a simple introduction to the roles played by different types of word

Finding words

1 Find the first letter of the word you wish to look up.
2 Using the alphabet line, find the section in your dictionary which lists words starting with that letter.
3 Once you have found that section, use the guide words at the top of each page to show you whether or not you are on the right page. Look at the second and third letters in your word. Do they come between the second and third letters of the alphabet in the two guide words at the top? If they do, you are probably on the right page.
4 Look down the page until you find your word.

Using this dictionary for spelling

If you want to remember a spelling from the dictionary you can use this method:

- read the word and remember the spelling
- cover the word
- write the word without looking at it
- uncover the word and check it against the one you have written

Playing the 'dictionary game'

Take turns suggesting a word and letting the other person find it. Who's the quickest?

Key to symbols and grammatical terms

(n) This means that the word is a noun. A **noun** is the word that we use for an object or thing. You can find out more about nouns by looking through the dictionary and seeing which words are nouns.

(v) This means that the word is a verb. A **verb** is a word that describes an action, or when something is done. Look at the verbs in the dictionary to find out more about verbs.

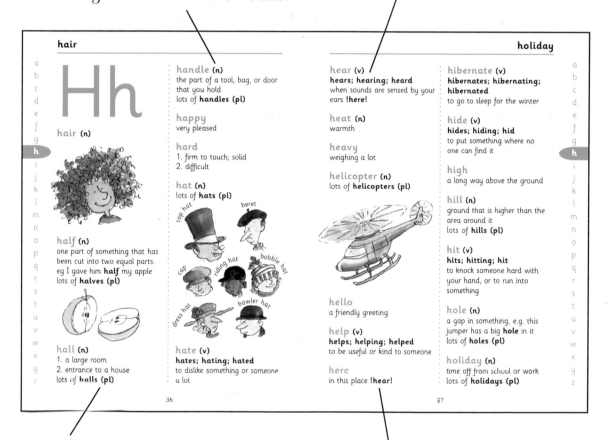

hair

Hh

hair (n)

half (n)
one part of something that has been cut into two equal parts:
eg I gave him **half** my apple
lots of **halves (pl)**

hall (n)
1. a large room
2. entrance to a house
lots of **halls (pl)**

handle (n)
the part of a tool, bag, or door that you hold
lots of **handles (pl)**

happy
very pleased

hard
1. firm to touch; solid
2. difficult

hat (n)
lots of **hats (pl)**

top hat   beret

cap   riding hat   bobble hat

dress hat   bowler hat

hate (v)
hates; hating; hated
to dislike something or someone
a lot

36

hear (v)
hears; hearing; heard
when sounds are sensed by your ears **!here!**

heat (n)
warmth

heavy
weighing a lot

helicopter (n)
lots of **helicopters (pl)**

hello
a friendly greeting

help (v)
helps; helping; helped
to be useful or kind to someone

here
in this place **!hear!**

holiday

hibernate (v)
hibernates; hibernating; hibernated
to go to sleep for the winter

hide (v)
hides; hiding; hid
to put something where no one can find it

high
a long way above the ground

hill (n)
ground that is higher than the area around it
lots of **hills (pl)**

hit (v)
hits; hitting; hit
to knock someone hard with your hand, or to run into something

hole (n)
a gap in something, e.g. this jumper has a big **hole** in it
lots of **holes (pl)**

holiday (n)
time off from school or work
lots of **holidays (pl)**

37

(pl) This means **plural**. When there is more than one noun. Most plural words are made by adding s to the end of the word, but some plurals have different spellings so watch out!

!! We've used these symbols to show you when to watch out for the spelling of a word. Two words that sound the same can have different spellings.

5

Aa

above

higher than something else
see page 112

abroad

in or to another country, e.g. I
go **abroad** on holiday

absent

not here, away

accident (n)

something which happens by
chance, often something bad
lots of **accidents (pl)**

ache (n)

(say ake) a pain which goes on
a long time
lots of **aches (pl)**

acorn (n)

the nut of the oak tree
lots of **acorns (pl)**

across

on or to the other side

act (v)
acts; acting; acted
to play a part, to pretend;
actor

add (v)
adds; adding; added
to put things together to make
more, often numbers

address (n)

the building in which
someone lives or works
lots of **addresses (pl)**

adult (n)

a grown-up person or animal
lots of **adults (pl)**

adventure (n)

an exciting journey or
holiday, sometimes
dangerous
lots of **adventures (pl)**

advertise (v)
advertises; advertising;
advertised
to tell lots of people about a
product or service

afraid
scared of something

after
being later or behind
something else

again
once more

age **(n)**
how old something is
lots of **ages** **(pl)**

agree **(v)**
agrees; agreeing; agreed
to think the same about
something as others do

air **(n)**
what we breathe to live
lots of **air** **(pl)**

airport **(n)**
a place where planes fly to
and from
lots of **airports** **(pl)**

alarm **(n)**
a warning given by a noise or
signal; **alarm clock**
lots of **alarms** **(pl)**

alive
to be living

all
everyone or everything

alone
without others

alphabet **(n)**
the set of letters used for
a language
lots of **alphabets** **(pl)**

altogether
completely

always
for ever

anchor **(n)**
lots of **anchors** **(pl)**

angel (n)
lots of **angels (pl)**

angry
very cross

animal (n)
lots of **animals (pl)**
see page 114

annoy (v)
annoys; annoying; annoyed
to make someone angry

another
1. one more of the same kind
2. a different one

answer (v)
answers; answering; answered
to respond to a question, letter or greeting

any
a number or amount; nothing in particular:
anybody, anyone, anything, anyway, anywhere

apologise (v)
apologises; apologising; apologised
to say sorry

appetite (n)
a want for food
lots of **appetites (pl)**

apron (n)
lots of **aprons (pl)**

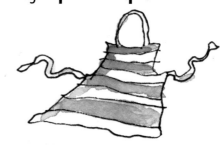

arch (n)
lots of **arches (pl)**

argue (v)
argues; arguing; argued
to have a disagreement

arithmetic (n)
number sums involving adding,
subtracting, multiplying and
dividing

armchair (n)
a chair with supports for
your arms
lots of **armchairs (pl)**

army (n)
a large number of people
trained to fight
lots of **armies (pl)**

arrive (v)
arrives; arriving; arrived
to reach a place

arrow (n)
1. a pointed stick shot from
a bow
2. a shape like this that shows
the way
lots of **arrows (pl)**

art (n)
a painting, drawing, statue or
other work created by an artist

ask (v)
asks; asking; asked
to make a request, e.g. he **asks**
for a sandwich

athletics (n)
sports including running and
jumping
lots of **athletics (pl)**

atlas (n)
a book of maps
lots of **atlases (pl)**

a
b
c
d
e
f
g
h
i
j
k
l
m
n
o
p
q
r
s
t
u
v
w
x
y
z

a
b
c
d
e
f
g
h
i
j
k
l
m
n
o
p
q
r
s
t
u
v
w
x
y
z

audience (n)

a group of people listening to or watching a performance

lots of **audiences (pl)**

automatic

a process or machine that works by itself with no human help

average

neither high nor low; in the middle

awake

not asleep (see page 112)

away

to go or be somewhere else

awful

horrible; shocking

Bb

baby (n)
a newly born child
lots of **babies (pl)**

back (n)
1. the rear part of a body between the shoulders and hips
2. the part furthest from the front
lots of **backs (pl)**

backwards
1. to go towards the back; to reverse
2. back to front

bacon (n)
slices of meat from a pig
lots of **bacon**

badge (n)
lots of **badges (pl)**

bag (n)
lots of **bags (pl)**

rucksack

handbag

briefcase

sports bag

bake (v)
bakes; baking; baked
to cook in an oven

balance (v)
balances; balancing; balanced
to have an even weight on each side; to keep steady

a
b
c
d
e
f
g
h
i
j
k
l
m
n
o
p
q
r
s
t
u
v
w
x
y
z

ball (n)
lots of **balls (pl)**

ballet (n)
a type of dance that tells a story

balloon (n)
lots of **balloons (pl)**

band (n)
1. a stripe or strip of material
2. a group of musicians
lots of **bands (pl)**

bank (n)
1. a place where money is kept
2. land along the side of a river
lots of **banks (pl)**

bark
1. **(n)** the outer part of a tree
lots of **bark (pl)**
2. **(v) barks; barking; barked**
to make a sharp, short sound, especially by a dog

basket (n)
lots of **baskets (pl)**

bat (n)
a stick, usually of wood, used to hit a ball
lots of **bats (pl)**

bath (n)
lots of **baths (pl)**

bathroom (n)
a room where people go to wash themselves
lots of **bathrooms (pl)**

battery (n)
a box for storing electricity
lots of **batteries (pl)**

be (v)
to exist: see page 124

beach (n)
the flat shore next to the sea
lots of **beaches (pl)**

bean (n)
the seed of some plants which can be eaten
!been! see page 121
lots of **beans (pl)**

beat
1. **(v) beats; beating; beat**
to win against someone else
2. **(n)** a regular rhythm
3. **(v)** to hit something

beautiful
lovely to look at

because
the reason for something

bed (n)
lots of **beds (pl)**

behave (v)
behaves; behaving; behaved
to act in a good or bad way;
behaviour

behind
not at the front; at the back

bell (n)
lots of **bells (pl)**

below
underneath: see page 112

a
b
c
d
e
f
g
h
i
j
k
l
m
n
o
p
q
r
s
t
u
v
w
x
y
z

bench (n)
a seat for more than one person
lots of **benches (pl)**

bend
1. **(v) bends; bending; bent**
to lean forwards
2. **(n)** a curve
lots of **bends (pl)**

best
(see good) as good as it
can be

big
of great size: large; **bigger;
biggest**

bin (n)
a container, especially for
rubbish
lots of **bins (pl)**

birth (n)
the moment someone is born;
birthday
lots of **births (pl)**

biscuit (n)
sweet pastry in a flat shape
lots of **biscuits (pl)**

bit (n)
a small part of something
lots of **bits (pl)**

bite (v)
bites; biting; bit
to take something between your
teeth **!byte!**

blind
1. not able to see
2. **(n)** a covering for a window
lots of **blinds (pl)**

blood (n)
the red liquid in our bodies
pumped by the heart; **bleed**
lots of **blood (pl)**

blow (v)
blows; blowing; blew
to force air out through the
mouth

board (n)
a flat piece of hard material, e.g. white**board**, chalk**board**, lots of **boards** (pl)

boat (n)
a floating vehicle
lots of **boats** (pl)

body (n)
lots of **bodies** (pl)
see page 116

bone (n)
lots of **bones** (pl)
see page 117

bonfire (n)
a large fire built outdoors
lots of **bonfires** (pl)

book (n)
lots of **books** (pl)

boot (n)
1. footwear which covers the foot and the lower leg
2. storage space at the back of a car
lots of **boots** (pl)

born
given life, e.g. I was **born** in 1990

bottle (n)
a tall glass or plastic container for liquid
lots of **bottles** (pl)

bounce (v)
bounces; bouncing; bounced
to spring back up from a hard surface

bowl
1. **(n)** a deep open container
lots of **bowls (pl)**
2. **(v) bowls; bowling; bowled**
to throw a ball in some games

box (n)
lots of **boxes (pl)**

brake (n)
something to stop a moving vehicle **!break!**
lots of **brakes (pl)**

bread (n)
a food made from flour

break
1. **(v) breaks; breaking; broke**
to make something come apart
2. **(n)** a short pause in an activity **!brake!**
lots of breaks **(pl)**

breakfast (n)
the first meal of the day
lots of **breakfasts (pl)**

breathe (v)
breathes; breathing; breathed
to take air into the body and let it out

brick (n)
a hard block of clay used for building
lots of **bricks (pl)**

bridge (n)
lots of **bridges (pl)**

bring (v)
brings; bringing; brought
to carry something with you;
brought (say brawt)

broom (n)
a brush with a long handle
lots of **brooms (pl)**

brush (n)
lots of **brushes (pl)**

bubble (n)
a hollow ball of liquid filled
with air
lots of **bubbles (pl)**

bucket (n)
lots of **buckets (pl)**

build (v)
builds; building; built
to make a house or wall by
putting pieces together

burst (v)
bursts; bursting; burst
to break suddenly because of
inside pressure, e.g. the
balloon **burst** suddenly

butter (n)
a paste made from milk used as
a spread and in cooking
lots of **butter**

button (n)
lots of **buttons (pl)**

a
b
c
d
e
f
g
h
i
j
k
l
m
n
o
p
q
r
s
t
u
v
w
x
y
z

a
b
c
d
e
f
g
h
i
j
k
l
m
n
o
p
q
r
s
t
u
v
w
x
y
z

Cc

café (n)
(say caffay) a place where you sit at a table and have a drink or a meal
lots of **cafés (pl)**

cage (n)
a metal container to keep animals in
lots of **cages (pl)**

calculator (n)
a machine for doing sums
lots of **calculators (pl)**

call (v)
calls; calling; called
1. to shout out
2. to telephone someone

camera (n)
a machine for taking photographs or making films
lots of **cameras (pl)**

candle (n)
lots of **candles (pl)**

capital
1. a large letter, such as A, B, C
2. the main city of a country

card (n)
1. stiff paper
lots of **card**
2. stiff paper, decorated and sent as a greeting, e.g. birthday **card**
lots of **cards (pl)**

cardboard (n)
thick stiff paper used for making boxes
lots of **cardboard (pl)**

cartoon (n)
a funny drawing; a film made using funny drawings
lots of **cartoons (pl)**

case (n)
a container for moving things: suit**case**; packing **case**
lots of **cases (pl)**

castle (n)
lots of **castles (pl)**

catch (v)
catches; catching; caught
to get hold of something

caterpillar (n)
lots of **caterpillars (pl)**

centre (n)
1. the middle
2. the main meeting place for one activity, e.g. business **centre**
lots of **centres (pl)**

cereal (n)
1. a grain such as wheat, oats, rice
2. a breakfast food made from some of the above

chain

chain (n)
lots of **chains (pl)**

chair (n)
lots of **chairs (pl)**

chalk (n)
1. a soft, crumbly rock
lots of **chalk**
2. sticks of the above used
for drawing
lots of **chalks (pl)**

change
1. **(v) changes; changing;
changed** to make something
different
2. **(n)** money given back when
you pay too much

cheap
not costing a lot

cheat (v)
cheats; cheating; cheated
to be dishonest

cheese (n)
a food made from milk

cheddar

swiss

edam

stilton

brie

child (n)
a small boy or girl
lots of **children (pl)**

chip (n)
a fried stick of potato
lots of **chips (pl)**

chocolate (n)
sweet food made with cocoa,
sugar and milk

a b c d e f g h i j k l m n o p q r s t u v w x y z

choice (n)
when you choose between one thing and another
lots of **choices (pl)**

choose (v)
chooses; choosing; chose
to pick one thing rather than another

church (n)
lots of **churches (pl)**

cinema (n)
a place where films are shown
lots of **cinemas (n)**

circus (n)
a show with performers, often in a tent
lots of **circuses (pl)**

city (n)
a large important town
lots of **cities (pl)**

clap (v)
claps; clapping; clapped
hit your hands together to make a noise

class (n)
a group of people taught together; **classroom**
lots of **classes (pl)**

clean
not dirty

clever
quick to learn

climb (v)
climbs; climbing; climbed
to go up something, e.g. I **climb** mountains

clock (n)
instrument for telling the time
lots of **clocks (pl)**

clothes (n)
things to wear

a b c d e f g h i j k l m n o p q r s t u v w x y z

a
b
c
d
e
f
g
h
i
j
k
l
m
n
o
p
q
r
s
t
u
v
w
x
y
z

cloud (n)
the fluffy patches in the sky
that rain comes from
lots of **clouds (pl)**

clown (n)
a performer who makes you laugh
lots of **clowns (pl)**

club (n)
a group of people with the same
interests
lots of **clubs (pl)**

coat (n)
a piece of clothing worn
outdoors over other clothes
lots of **coats (pl)**

blazer

overcoat

anorak

raincoat

jacket

coffee (n)
a drink made from coffee beans
lots of **coffee**

coin (n)
a metal disc used as money
lots of **coins (pl)**

cold
1. not having heat
2. **(n)** a common illness
lots of **colds (pl)**

colour (n)
see page 111
lots of **colours (pl)**

comic (n)
a magazine with stories in pictures
lots of **comics (pl)**

concert (n)
a musical performance for an audience
lots of **concerts (pl)**

consonant (n)
a letter of the alphabet other than a, e, i, o or u
(see vowel)
many **consonants (pl)**

control (v)
controls; controlling; controlled
to have power over something;
remote control

cook (v)
cooks; cooking; cooked
to heat food for eating

cool
a little bit cold: not hot

copy (v)
copies; copying; copied
to make something exactly the same

corner (n)
where two lines or roads meet
lots of **corners (pl)**

cost (n)
what you pay for something
lots of **costs (pl)**

cot (n)
a bed for a baby
lots of **cots (pl)**

cough (n)
(say kof) sickness that makes your throat tickle
lots of **coughs (pl)**

count (v)
counts; counting; counted
to find out how many there are

country (n)
1. a land with its own government
lots of **countries (pl)**
2. land outside towns and cities:
countryside

crash (n)
1. a loud noise
2. a vehicle accident
lots of **crashes (pl)**

crisps (n)
thin slices of fried potato
lots of **crisps (pl)**

cross
upset about something

cry (v)
cries; crying; cried
to have tears coming from your eyes

cup (n)
lots of **cups (pl)**

cupboard (n)
lots of **cupboards (pl)**

curtain (n)
material hung to cover windows
lots of **curtains (pl)**

cushion (n)
a soft padded cloth used to make seats more comfortable
lots of **cushions (pl)**

custard (n)
a sweet yellow sauce
lots of **custard (pl)**

cut (v)
cuts; cutting; cut
to slice with something sharp

Dd

daisy (n)
lots of **daisies (pl)**

dance (v)
dances; dancing; danced
to move to music

dangerous
not safe

dark
having no light

date (n)
which day, month and year it is
lots of **dates (pl)**

dead
not living; **death; die; dying**

deaf
not able to hear

dear
1. much loved
2. costing a lot

den (n)
1. a private place
2. home of a wild animal
lots of **dens (pl)**

dentist (n)
a person who takes care of
your teeth
lots of **dentists (pl)**

desk (n)
a table for writing
lots of **desks (pl)**

diamond (n)
a jewel (also a shape)
lots of **diamonds (pl)**

diary (n)
a book for writing about
each day
lots of **diaries (pl)**

a
b
c
d
e
f
g
h
i
j
k
l
m
n
o
p
q
r
s
t
u
v
w
x
y
z

a
b
c
d
e
f
g
h
i
j
k
l
m
n
o
p
q
r
s
t
u
v
w
x
y
z

dice (n)
counting cubes for games

dictionary (n)
a book giving the meanings and spellings of words
lots of **dictionaries (pl)**

different
not the same

difficult
hard to do or understand

dig (v)
digs; digging; dug
to make a hole in earth

dinner (n)
a main meal, eaten at midday or in the evening
lots of **dinners (pl)**

dinosaur (n)
reptiles that lived millions of years ago
lots of **dinosaurs (pl)**

Tyrannosaurus

Diplodocus

Triceratops

dirty
anything that is not clean

discover (v)
discovers; discovering; discovered
to find or find out about something

dive
entering water head first

doctor (n)

a person who looks after sick people
lots of **doctors (pl)**

doll (n)

lots of **dolls (pl)**

door (n)

the way in to a room or building
lots of **doors (pl)**

dragon (n)

lots of **dragons (pl)**

draw (v)

draws; drawing; drew

to make pictures

drawer (n)

a box inside a cupboard to keep things in
lots of **drawers (pl)**

dream (n)

things you imagine, usually when asleep
lots of **dreams (pl)**

dress (n)

lots of **dresses (pl)**

drink (v)

drinks; drinking; drank; drunk

to swallow liquids

drive (v)

drives; driving; drove

to make a vehicle go where you want it

dry

not damp or wet

Ee

a
b
c
d
e
f
g
h
i
j
k
l
m
n
o
p
q
r
s
t
u
v
w
x
y
z

early
before or at the start of a period of time, e.g. **early** in the morning

earth (n)
1. soil
lots of **earth**
2. **Earth**: the planet we live on

easy
not difficult

eat (v)
eats; eating; ate
to chew and swallow food

education (n)
what we are taught and learn
lots of **education**

egg (n)
lots of **eggs (pl)**

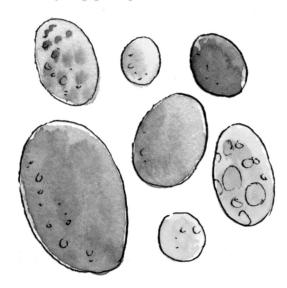

elastic (n)
a stretchy material
lots of **elastic**

empty
having nothing inside

energy (n)
power
lots of **energy**

enjoy (v)
enjoys; enjoying; enjoyed
to get pleasure from something

a
b
c
d
e
f
g
h
i
j
k
l
m
n
o
p
q
r
s
t
u
v
w
x
y
z

enough
(say eenuff) as much as needed

envelope (n)
a paper container for a
letter or card
lots of **envelopes (pl)**

escape (v)
escapes; escaping; escaped
to get away

evening (n)
the part of the day between
afternoon and night
lots of **evenings (pl)**

every
each one; all; **everybody,**
everyone, everything,
everywhere

example (n)
shows the way a thing should
be done, e.g. set an **example**
lots of **examples (pl)**

exciting
interesting and thrilling

exercise (v)
exercises; exercising;
exercised
to move your body to keep it fit

stretch
bend

run

jog

expensive
costing a lot

explain (v)
explains; explaining;
explained
to help another person to
understand

Ff

a
b
c
d
e
f
g
h
i
j
k
l
m
n
o
p
q
r
s
t
u
v
w
x
y
z

face (n)
lots of **faces** (pl)

fact (n)
something that is true
lots of facts **(pl)**

fair
1. treating people equally
2. **(n)** a show with rides and
games, lots of **fairs** (pl)

fall (v)
falls; falling; fell
to drop down

family (n)
people who are related to you
see page 118
lots of **families** (pl)

famous
well known by many people

fan (n)
lots of **fans** (pl)

farm (n)
land and buildings for
keeping animals and
growing food
lots of **farms** (pl)

fat
1. **(n)** a white greasy product
that comes from animals
2. not slim

favourite
the one liked best

fear (n)
being afraid of something
lots of **fears (pl)**

feather (n)
lots of **feathers (pl)**

feed (v)
feeds; feeding; fed
to give food to

feel (v)
feels; feeling; felt
to touch

felt (n)
thick woollen cloth; **felt-tip pen**

fence (n)
lots of **fences (pl)**

field (n)
open land often surrounded by
a fence, hedge or wall
lots of **fields (pl)**

fill (v)
fills; filling; filled
to put things into a container
until **full**

film (n)
1. a story told in moving pictures
on television or at the cinema
2. material used in cameras to
take photographs

find (v)
finds; finding; found
to come across something

finish (v)
**finishes; finishing;
finished**
to get to the end of something;
to stop

a
b
c
d
e
f
g
h
i
j
k
l
m
n
o
p
q
r
s
t
u
v
w
x
y
z

a
b
c
d
e
f
g
h
i
j
k
l
m
n
o
p
q
r
s
t
u
v
w
x
y
z

fire (n)
a burning pile of material
lots of **fires (pl)**

fit
1. **(v) fits; fitting; fitted**
to be the correct size
2. healthy

fix (v)
fixes; fixing; fixed
to mend

flag (n)
lots of **flags (pl)**

Great Britain   U.S.A

France   Japan

flavour (n)
the taste of something
lots of **flavours (pl)**

flood (n)
water covering a place that is usually dry
lots of **floods (pl)**

flour (n)
powder used for making bread
!flower!

flower (n)
!flour! lots of **flowers (pl)**

daisy   bluebell   lavender   tulip   rose

fly
1.**(v) flies; flying; flew**
to travel through the air
2. **(n)** an insect that flies
lots of **flies (pl)**

fog (n)
thick mist

fold (v)
folds; folding; folded
to bend paper or fabric so that it is tidy or takes up less space

follow (v)
follows; following; followed
to go after something

food (n)
something to eat
lots of **food**

football (n)
1. a team game played with
a ball
2. the ball used for playing
this game, lots of **footballs (pl)**

forest (n)
a large area of trees
lots of **forests (pl)**

forget (v)
forgets; forgetting; forgot
to not remember

fork (n)
a metal tool that you eat with
lots of **forks (pl)**

forward
towards the front

free
1. costing nothing
2. able to do anything or
go anywhere

freezer (n)
a machine to keep things frozen
lots of **freezers (pl)**

fridge (n)
a machine to keep things cold
lots of **fridges (pl)**

friend (n)
someone you like a lot
lots of **friends (pl)**

front
the most forward part of
something

fruit (n)
see page 120

fry (v)
fries; frying; fried
to cook in hot fat

full
holding as much as possible

fun (n)
something that makes us laugh;
funny
lots of **fun (pl)**

fur (n)
the soft hair of animals

Gg

a
b
c
d
e
f
g
h
i
j
k
l
m
n
o
p
q
r
s
t
u
v
w
x
y
z

game (n)
a competition or sport that you play, often with other people, such as chess; ludo; football
lots of **games (pl)**

garage (n)
a building by a house where cars are kept, or a shop where they are mended
lots of **garages (pl)**

garden (n)
land, often round a house, where flowers and other plants are grown
lots of **gardens (pl)**

gate (n)
lots of **gates (pl)**

giant
much larger than usual, e.g. James and the **Giant** Peach

gift (n)
a present
lots of **gifts (pl)**

girl (n)
a female child
lots of **girls (pl)**

glass (n)
1. hard, see-through material used in windows, lots of **glass**
2. something to drink out of, made from this material
lots of **glasses (pl)**

glove (n)
material covers for the hands
a pair of **gloves (pl)**

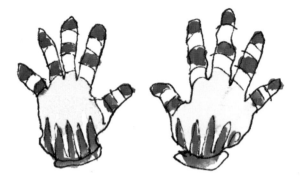

glue (n)
a liquid which sticks things
together

goal (n)
lots of **goals (pl)**
goalposts

gold (n)
a valuable yellow metal used
for jewellery

good
1. useful or suitable; **better,
best**
2. well behaved

grass (n)
a green plant used to cover
large areas

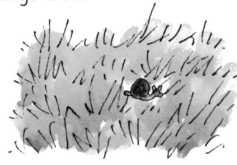

great
large or important

ground (n)
the surface of the Earth

group (n)
several people or things together
lots of **groups (pl)**

grow (v)
grows; growing; grew
to get bigger

guess (v)
guesses; guessing; guessed
to say what you think, without
knowing for certain

a
b
c
d
e
f
g
h
i
j
k
l
m
n
o
p
q
r
s
t
u
v
w
x
y
z

a
b
c
d
e
f
g
h
i
j
k
l
m
n
o
p
q
r
s
t
u
v
w
x
y
z

Hh

hair (n)

half (n)

one part of something that has been cut into two equal parts: e.g. I gave him **half** my apple
lots of **halves (pl)**

hall (n)

1. a large room
2. entrance to a house
lots of **halls (pl)**

handle (n)

the part of a tool, bag, or door that you hold
lots of **handles (pl)**

happy

very pleased

hard

1. firm to touch; solid
2. difficult

hat (n)

lots of **hats (pl)**

top hat

beret

cap

riding hat

bobble hat

dress hat

bowler hat

hate (v)

hates; hating; hated

to dislike something or someone a lot

hear (v)
hears; hearing; heard
when sounds are sensed by your ears !**here!**

heat (n)
warmth
lots of **heat**

heavy
weighing a lot

helicopter (n)
lots of **helicopters** (pl)

hello
a friendly greeting

help (v)
helps; helping; helped
to be useful or kind to someone

here
in this place !**hear!**

hibernate (v)
hibernates; hibernating; hibernated
to go to sleep for the winter

hide (v)
hides; hiding; hid
to put something where no one can find it

high
a long way above the ground

hill (n)
ground that is higher than the area around it
lots of **hills** (pl)

hit (v)
hits; hitting; hit
to knock someone hard with your hand, or to run into something

hole (n)
a gap in something, e.g. this jumper has a big **hole** in it
lots of **holes** (pl)

holiday (n)
time off from school or work
lots of **holidays** (pl)

a
b
c
d
e
f
g
h
i
j
k
l
m
n
o
p
q
r
s
t
u
v
w
x
y
z

home

a
b
c
d
e
f
g
h
i
j
k
l
m
n
o
p
q
r
s
t
u
v
w
x
y
z

home (n)
where you live
lots of **homes** (pl)

hood (n)
lots of **hoods** (pl)

hook (n)
curved metal for hanging
things up
lots of **hooks** (pl)

hop (v)
hops; hopping; hopped
to jump on one leg

hope (v)
hopes; hoping; hoped
to wish for and expect something

horrible
not nice

hospital (n)
where sick people get better
lots of **hospitals** (pl)

hot
very warm

house (n)
lots of **houses** (pl)

hug (v)
hugs; hugging; hugged
to put your arms round
someone

huge
very large

hungry
in need of food

hurry (v)
hurries; hurrying; hurried
to go quickly

Ii

ice (n)
frozen water

ice cream (n)
a sweet frozen pudding, usually made from cream

idea (n)
a thought about something to do or make
lots of **ideas (pl)**

ill
not well; **illness,** sickness

illustration (n)
a picture of something in a book
lots of **illustrations (pl)**

imagine (v)
imagines; imagining; imagined
to picture something in your mind

impatient
when you can't wait for something to happen

important
something that matters a lot

impossible
something that cannot be done

indoors
inside a building

initial (n)
the first letter of a name
lots of **initials (pl)**

injection (n)
when someone gives you medicine with a needle in your skin
lots of **injections (pl)**

injure (v)
injures; injuring; injured
to hurt; **injury**

a b c d e f g h i j k l m n o p q r s t u v w x y z

insect

insect (n)
a small creature with six legs
lots of **insects (pl)**

bee
butterfly
ladybird
fly
wasp
ant
moth

inside
the part within something else

instead
in place of something or someone

instrument (n)
1. a tool
2. a thing played to make music
lots of **instruments (pl)**

trumpet
guitar
drum

interest (v)
interests; interesting; interested
wanting to know about
something; **interested**

interrupt (v)
interrupts; interrupting; interrupted
to talk while someone else is
already speaking; to stop
something from carrying on

invite (v)
invites; inviting; invited
to ask someone to come to
something, e.g. a party

iron (n)
1. a tool that makes clothes
smooth
2. a type of metal
lots of **irons (pl)**

island (n)
land surrounded by water
lots of **islands (pl)**

itch (n)
a feeling that makes you want
to scratch; **itchy**
lots of **itches (pl)**

jacket (n)
a short coat
lots of **jackets (pl)**

jam (n)
a sweet, fruity spread often eaten with bread

jar (n)
a short, glass container
lots of **jars (pl)**

jeans (n)
trousers made of denim material, often blue

jelly (n)
a soft pudding that wobbles
lots of **jellies (pl)**

jet (n)
a type of plane
lots of **jets (pl)**

jewel (n)
an expensive stone used in jewellery
lots of **jewels (pl)**

a
b
c
d
e
f
g
h
i
j
k
l
m
n
o
p
q
r
s
t
u
v
w
x
y
z

a
b
c
d
e
f
g
h
i
j
k
l
m
n
o
p
q
r
s
t
u
v
w
x
y
z

jigsaw (n)
a picture, cut into small pieces, which are then put back together as a puzzle
lots of **jigsaws (pl)**

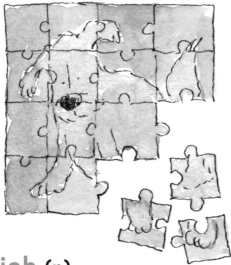

job (n)
another name for work
lots of **jobs (pl)**

join (v)
joins; joining; joined
1. to fix together
2. become part of a group

joke (n)
something you say to make people laugh
lots of **jokes (pl)**

journey (n)
a trip over a long distance
lots of **journeys (pl)**

jug (n)
a thing like a big cup, with a spout, that pours water or other drinks
lots of **jugs (pl)**

milk jug

measuring jug

cream jug

juice (n)
the liquid that comes out of fruit

jump (v)
jumps; jumping; jumped
to spring up from the ground

Kk

keep (v)
keeps; keeping; kept
to save something for yourself

ketchup (n)
a sauce usually made from
tomatoes
lots of **ketchup**

kettle (n)
a pot for heating water
lots of **kettles (pl)**

key (n)
a shaped piece of metal for
unlocking doors
a bunch of **keys (pl)**

kick (v)
kicks; kicking; kicked
to hit with a foot

kind
helpful and nice

king (n)
the crowned male ruler of
a country
lots of **kings (pl)**

a b c d e f g h i j **k** l m n o p q r s t u v w x y z

kiss

kiss (v)
kisses; kissing; kissed
to touch with the lips

kitchen (n)
the room where food is cooked
lots of **kitchens (pl)**

kite (n)
a toy that is blown by the wind
when you hold it by a string
lots of **kites (pl)**

kneel (v)
kneels; kneeling; knelt
to go down on your knees

knickers (n)
underpants, usually for girls
lots of **knickers (pl)**

knife (n)
a sharp tool for cutting
lots of **knives (pl)**

knot (n)
a tangled lump made by tying
up string or fabric
lots of **knots (pl)**

know (v)
knows; knowing; knew
to have learned, e.g. I **know**
how to tell the time

Ll

ladder (n)
a thing with steps that you climb up to get to high places
lots of **ladders (pl)**

lady (n)
a polite word for a grown-up female
lots of **ladies (pl)**

ladybird (n)
a red insect with black spots
lots of **ladybirds (pl)**

lake (n)
a large pool of water surrounded by land
lots of **lakes (pl)**

land (n)
the dry part of the Earth's surface

language (n)
words we use to speak and write
lots of **languages (pl)**

large
big

a
b
c
d
e
f
g
h
i
j
k
l
m
n
o
p
q
r
s
t
u
v
w
x
y
z

last

a
b
c
d
e
f
g
h
i
j
k
l
m
n
o
p
q
r
s
t
u
v
w
x
y
z

last
at the end

late
after the expected time

laugh (v)
laughs; laughing; laughed
to make a sound because you
are happy

lazy
not wanting to work

lead (v)
leads; leading; led
to go first

leaf (n)
the green part of a tree
or plant
lots of **leaves (pl)**

learn (v)
learns; learning; learned
to find out about

least
the smallest amount, e.g. I have
the **least** lemonade

leave (v)
leaves; leaving; left
to go away from

left
the side opposite to right

lemonade (n)
a drink made from lemons,
usually fizzy

length (n)
how long something is

less
not as much as someone else,
e.g. I have **less** milk than him

lesson (n)
a time when someone teaches you
lots of **lessons (pl)**

letter (n)
1. one of the symbols that we use to make up words, see **alphabet**
2. a written message to someone
lots of **letters (pl)**

library (n)
a room or building containing many books
lots of **libraries (pl)**

lick (v)
licks; licking; licked
to wet with the tongue

lid (n)
a cover for a jar or pot
lots of **lids (pl)**

lie (v)
1. **lies; lying; lied**
to say something not true
2. **lies; lying; lay**
to have your body flat, e.g. on a bed

life (n)
the time between the birth and death of a plant or animal
lots of **lives (pl)**

lift (v)
1. **(v) lifts; lifting; lifted**
to pick up
2. **(n)** a machine which moves people or things between floors in a building
lots of **lifts (pl)**

light
1. not heavy
2. bright, like daytime

lightning (n)
a flash of light in the sky when there is a thunderstorm
lots of **lightning**

a b c d e f g h i j k l m n o p q r s t u v w x y z

47

like

like
1. **(v) likes; liking; liked** to be fond of something or someone
2. similar, e.g. he looks **like** you

line **(n)**
1. a thin drawn mark
2. a row of people or things
lots of **lines (pl)**

lip **(n)**
one of the two parts round your mouth
a pair of **lips (pl)**

liquid **(n)**
a wet substance that can be poured, e.g. water, milk, petrol

list **(n)**
things written down one after another, e.g. **shopping list**
lots of **lists (pl)**

listen **(v)**
listens; listening; listened
to try to hear

litter **(n)**
rubbish which is left lying around
lots of **litter**

little
small

live **(v)**
lives; living; lived
to have life

loaf **(n)**
a piece of bread
lots of **loaves (pl)**

tin loaf

cob

bloomer

lock
1. **(v) locks; locking; locked**
to close with a key
2. **(n)** the hole, often in a door, where the key goes in to lock and unlock the door
lots of **locks (pl)**

log (n)
a thick, rounded piece of wood
lots of **logs (pl)**

lollipop (n)
a sweet on a stick
lots of **lollipops (pl)**

lonely
unhappy because you are on your own

long
a great distance or amount of time

look (v)
looks; looking; looked
to use your eyes to see something

lose (v)
loses, losing, lost
1. to be unable to find something
2. to not win something, e.g. a race

loud
noisy

love (v)
loves; loving; loved
to like someone very much

lovely
very nice; good to look at

low
near the ground

luck (n)
a good thing which happens to you: **lucky**
lots of **luck**

lunch (n)
the midday meal

a
b
c
d
e
f
g
h
i
j
k
l
m
n
o
p
q
r
s
t
u
v
w
x
y
z

Mm

machine (n)
an instrument that does a
particular job
lots of **machines (pl)**

magic
things which happen, that cannot
be explained; e.g. **magic** trick

magnet (n)
a special piece of metal that is
able to pull other metal things
towards it
lots of **magnets (pl)**

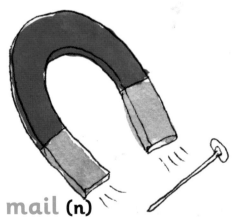

mail (n)
letters and parcels received
through the post **!male!**
lots of **mail**

make (v)
makes; making; made
to build or create something

man (n)
a male adult
lots of **men (pl)**

many
lots, e.g. **many** men play
football

map (n)
a plan of an area, e.g. city,
country
lots of **maps (pl)**

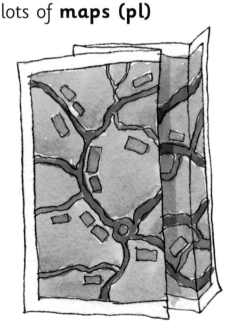

mark (v)
marks; marking; marked
to put a sign on something, e.g.
the teacher **marked** my book

market (n)
a place where you go to buy
and sell things
lots of **markets (pl)**

marry (v)
marries; marrying; married
to become the husband or wife
of someone

mat (n)
material for covering part of a
floor or table
lots of **mats (pl)**

match (n)
1. something which goes with
something else exactly, e.g. a
perfect **match**
2. a game for two teams
3. a small stick that
produces a flame
lots of **matches (pl)**

mathematics (n)
using numbers to do sums and
solve problems

mattress (n)
the soft part of a bed that you
sleep on
lots of **mattresses (pl)**

maybe
perhaps

meal (n)
breakfast, lunch or dinner
lots of **meals (pl)**

measure (v)
**measures; measuring;
measured**
to find the size of something

a b c d e f g h i j k l **m** n o p q r s t u v w x y z

51

meat

a
b
c
d
e
f
g
h
i
j
k
l
m
n
o
p
q
r
s
t
u
v
w
x
y
z

meat (n)
parts of an animal that are
eaten !**meet**!

medicine (n)
something you take when you
are ill to make you feel better

meet (v)
meets; meeting; met
to get together with other
people ! **meat** !

memory (n)
a thing that happened in the
past that we remember
lots of **memories (pl)**

mess (n)
a group of things that are
untidy or not under control

microwave (n)
an oven for cooking food
very quickly
lots of **microwave ovens (pl)**

middle
the place that is the same
distance from two ends

might
when something is possible,
e.g. the jam **might** be on
the shelf

milk (n)
a white liquid that comes from
mothers to feed their young
lots of **milk**

mince (n)
meat cut into very small pieces

mind

1. **(n)** your memory and thoughts
lots of **minds (pl)**
2. **(v) minds; minding; minded**
to be careful of something

mirror **(n)**

glass which can reflect things
lots of **mirrors (pl)**

miss **(v)**

misses; missing; missed
1. to fail to hit something
2. to feel unhappy because something or someone is not there

mistake **(n)**

something that is wrong
lots of **mistakes (pl)**

mix **(v)**

mixes; mixing; mixed
to put things together to make something new

mobile **(n)**

a phone that you carry around
lots of **mobiles (pl)**

model **(n)**

an example, or way of showing how something will look, e.g. a fashion model
lots of **models (pl)**

money **(n)**

what we use to pay for things
lots of money

monster **(n)**

a frightening creature in stories
lots of **monsters (pl)**

a b c d e f g h i j k l m n o p q r s t u v w x y z

moon (n)
a large bright shape in the
night sky
lots of **moons (pl)**

more
a bigger amount

morning (n)
the time before noon/midday
lots of **mornings (pl)**

mountain (n)
a very high hill
lots of **mountains (pl)**

mouth (n)
part of your face which is used
to eat and speak with
lots of **mouths (pl)**

move (v)
moves; moving; moved
to go from one place to another

much
a great deal

mud (n)
very wet soil
lots of mud

music (n)
special patterns of sound made
by singers or instruments
lots of **music**

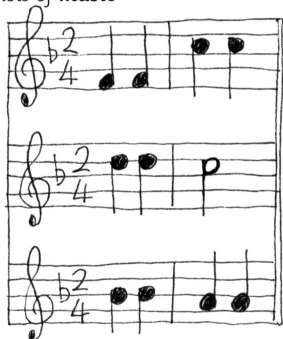

must
when someone really has to do
something, e.g. I **must** clean
my teeth every day.

Nn

nail (n)
1. the hard cover found at the ends of your fingers and toes

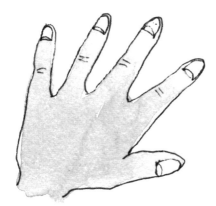

2. a small metal thing which is hammered into wood
lots of **nails (pl)**

name (n)
what something or someone is called
lots of **names (pl)**

nature (n)
things in the world all around us that live and grow

naughty
doing things that are bad or not allowed

near
close by

nearly
almost

need (v)
needs; needing; needed
when you must have something

neighbour (n)
someone living near you
lots of **neighbours (pl)**

nervous
a bit worried

nest (n)
a home built by birds and some animals
lots of **nests (pl)**

never
not at any time

new
not used before

news (n)
information about what is happening

next
following on

nice
good to see, hear or taste; kind

night (n)
the part of the day when it is dark
lots of **nights (pl)**

nobody
no person; no one

noise (n)
a sound or sounds that are often loud and not very nice

none
not any

note (n)
1. a short written message
2. a single musical sound
lots of **notes (pl)**

nothing
not a thing; zero

now
at this time

nurse (n)
a person who looks after sick people
lots of **nurses (pl)**

Oo

object (n)
a solid thing
lots of **objects (pl)**

ocean (n)
a very large sea
lots of **oceans (pl)**

o'clock
telling the time on the hour

often
many times

oil (n)
a natural liquid often used for
cooking or fuel

old
not young or new

once
something that happens a single
time

only
one and no more

opposite
as different as possible to
something

orchestra (n)
a large group of musicians
playing different instruments
lots of **orchestras (pl)**

cymbals

double bass

trumpet

violin

clarinet

a b c d e f g h i j k l m n **o** p q r s t u v w x y z

a
b
c
d
e
f
g
h
i
j
k
l
m
n
o
p
q
r
s
t
u
v
w
x
y
z

order (n)
1. a request for something
2. when you are told you must do something
3. the way things are arranged

ordinary
normal or usual; nothing different

ostrich (n)
a big fast running bird
lots of **ostriches (pl)**

other
a different one

otter (n)
a furry animal with webbed feet
lots of **otters (pl)**

our
belonging to us

out
not in a building or at home

outside (n)
1. the edge of something
2. not in a building

oven (n)
a place, often like a square box, where the air is made so hot that it can cook and heat food
lots of **ovens (pl)**

own
1. **(v) owns; owning; owned**
to have something which belongs to you
2. to be alone, e.g. on your **own**

Pp

packet (n)
a small parcel or bag
lots of **packets (pl)**

page (n)
one side of a sheet of paper;
e.g. this is on page 59
lots of **pages (pl)**

pain (n)
a feeling of hurting

paint (n)
a thick coloured liquid used for
making pictures or decorating

pair (n)
two things that go together
!pear!
lots of **pairs (pl)**

palace (n)
a very grand building
lots of **palaces (pl)**

pan (n)
a metal container used for
cooking
lots of **pans (pl)**

pancake (n)
a thin cake cooked in a
frying pan
lots of **pancakes (pl)**

pants (n)
underwear, knickers

paper (n)
a thin material used for
writing on

a b c d e f g h i j k l m n o **p** q r s t u v w x y z

a
b
c
d
e
f
g
h
i
j
k
l
m
n
o
p
q
r
s
t
u
v
w
x
y
z

park
1. **(n)** a large garden or grassy area for public use
lots of **parks (pl)**
2. **(v) parks; parking; parked** to leave a vehicle stopped

part **(n)**
a piece of something
lots of **parts (pl)**

partner **(n)**
a friend who does things with you
lots of **partners (pl)**

party **(n)**
a time when people have fun together
lots of **parties (pl)**

pass **(v)**
passes; passing; passed
1. to hand something to someone
2. to move by something or someone
3. to do well in a test or exam

past
1. everything that has already happened
2. to go by someone **!passed!**

paste **(n)**
a soft mixture

path **(n)**
a walkway
lots of **paths (pl)**

patient
1. **(n)** someone being treated for an illness
lots of **patients (pl)**
2. able to wait for something

pattern **(n)**
a sequence of colours, shapes or objects, sometimes made to look nice
lots of **patterns (pl)**

pavement **(n)**
a path by a road for people to walk on

paw **(n)**
an animal's foot, often with pads and claws
four **paws (pl)**

pay (v)
pays; paying; paid
to give money for something

peace (n)
quiet, still and calm **!piece!**

pedal (n)
the part of a bicycle you push
with your foot to make it move
lots of **pedals (pl)**

peg (n)
1. a small knob for hanging
coats on

2. a clip for hanging
washing on a line
lots of **pegs (pl)**

pen (n)
a tool for writing with ink
lots of **pens (pl)**

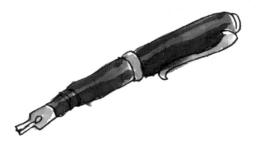

pencil (n)
a tool for writing and drawing
using graphite
lots of **pencils (pl)**

penny (n)
a small coin: there are
one hundred of these in
a British pound
lots of **pennies (pl)**

people (n)
human beings

performance (n)
a theatre, film or TV show done
in front of an audience
lots of **performances (pl)**

a b c d e f g h i j k l m n o **p** q r s t u v w x y z

perhaps

a
b
c
d
e
f
g
h
i
j
k
l
m
n
o
p
q
r
s
t
u
v
w
x
y
z

perhaps
what may be: possibly

person (n)
a single human being
lots of **people (pl)**

pet (n)
an animal you care for
and keep in the home
lots of **pets (pl)**

petal (n)
the colourful part of a flower
lots of **petals (pl)**

petrol (n)
liquid used to power a motor
engine

phone (n)
a thing you use to talk to
someone who is somewhere else;
short for 'telephone'
lots of **phones (pl)**

photograph (n)
a picture taken by a camera
lots of **photographs (pl)**

picnic (n)
a meal eaten outside
lots of **picnics (pl)**

picture (n)
a painting, drawing or
photograph
lots of **pictures (pl)**

pie (n)
food baked in a pastry case
lots of **pies (pl)**

piece (n)
a part of something bigger
! peace !
lots of **pieces (pl)**

pile (n)
things put in a heap
lots of **piles (pl)**

pillow (n)
a large soft cushion to rest your
head on in bed
lots of **pillows (pl)**

pin (n)
a small pointed metal stick that
holds things together
lots of **pins (pl)**

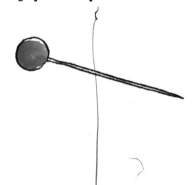

62

place (n)
an area or position
lots of **places (pl)**

plain
simple; not decorated

plant (n)
a living thing growing in the ground
lots of **plants (pl)**

plaster (n)
material stuck over a cut or graze to keep it clean
lots of **plasters (pl)**

plastic (n)
a man-made material

plate (n)
a flat dish for food
lots of **plates (pl)**

play
1. **(v) plays; playing; played**
to take part in a game
2. **(v)** to make sounds on musical instruments
3. **(n)** a story performed by actors
lots of **plays (pl)**

please
a word used to ask politely

pocket (n)
a bag sewn onto clothes to put things in
lots of **pockets (pl)**

poem (n)
writing in patterns of lines, often rhyming
lots of **poems (pl)**

point
1. **(n)** a sharp end, e.g. the point of a needle
lots of **points (pl)**
2. **(v) points; pointing; pointed**
to show direction with a finger

police (n)
people who make others obey the law

a b c d e f g h i j k l m n o p q r s t u v w x y z

polish (v)
polishes; polishing; polished
when you rub things to make them shiny

polite
having good manners

pond (n)
a pool of water, often in a garden
lots of **ponds (pl)**

pool (n)
water, often used for swimming
lots of **pools (pl)**

possible
it may happen

post
1. **(n)** a pole fixed in the ground
lots of **posts (pl)**
2. **(v) posts; posting; posted**
to send something by mail

poster (n)
a large picture or notice
lots of **posters (pl)**

pound (n)
a unit of money in Britain equal to 100 pence; £1
one hundred **pounds (pl)**

pour (v)
pours; pouring; poured
to make something flow from a container

powder (n)
very fine grains

power (n)
strength; energy

prepare (v)
prepares; preparing; prepared
to get ready

present (n)
a gift
lots of **presents** (pl)

pretend (v)
**pretends; pretending;
pretended**
to imagine that you are
someone or somewhere else

pretty
nice to look at

price (n)
the cost of something
lots of **prices** (pl)

prince (n)
the son of a king or queen
lots of **princes** (pl)

princess (n)
the daughter of a king or queen
lots of **princesses** (pl)

print (v)
prints; printing; printed
to make marks on paper, e.g. a
book is **printed**

prize (n)
a reward for doing well or
winning
lots of **prizes** (pl)

problem (n)
a difficulty; something
needing to be solved
lots of **problems** (pl)

programme (n)
a show on radio or television
! program !
lots of **programmes** (pl)

a
b
c
d
e
f
g
h
i
j
k
l
m
n
o
p
q
r
s
t
u
v
w
x
y
z

a
b
c
d
e
f
g
h
i
j
k
l
m
n
o
p
q
r
s
t
u
v
w
x
y
z

promise (v)
promises; promising; promised
to mean you will do as you say

pudding (n)
a sweet food eaten after a main meal
lots of **puddings (pl)**

puddle (n)
a small pool of water
lots of **puddles (pl)**

pull (v)
pulls; pulling; pulled
to move something towards you; the opposite of push

pupil (n)
someone being taught
lots of **pupils (pl)**

puppet (n)
a doll which moves by pulling strings or putting it on your hand
lots of **puppets (pl)**

purse (n)
a small bag that holds money
lots of **purses (pl)**

push (v)
pushes; pushing; pushed
to move something away from you; the opposite of pull

puzzle (n)
a game or problem that you do not understand
lots of **puzzles (pl)**

quality (n)
how good something is

quantity (n)
how much or how many there
are of something
lots of **quantities (pl)**

quarrel (n)
an argument
lots of **quarrels (pl)**

quarter (n)
one of four equal parts of
anything; $\frac{1}{4}$
four **quarters (pl)**

queen (n)
the female ruler of a country
lots of **queens (pl)**

question (n)
something you ask and want an
answer to
lots of **questions (pl)**

queue (n)
a line of waiting people
or cars
lots of **queues (pl)**

quick
fast

quiet
with little or no noise

quite
more than a little

quiz (n)
a game where
questions are asked
lots of **quizzes (pl)**

Rr

race (n)
a competition where people see
who is the fastest at something
lots of **races (pl)**

racket (n)
a type of bat with strings
lots of **rackets (pl)**

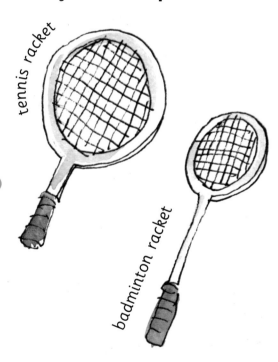

tennis racket

badminton racket

radiator (n)
an object used to heat a room
lots of **radiators (pl)**

radio (n)
a machine which we can listen
to that receives sound waves
through the air
lots of **radios (pl)**

railway (n)
a track for a train to run along
lots of **railways (pl)**

rain (n)
water falling in drops from
clouds

rainbow (n)
a band of seven colours seen in
the sky when it is sunny and
raining at the same time
lots of **rainbows (pl)**

rather
1. prefer to
2. quite: a bit

rattle (n)
a baby's toy that makes a noise
when shaken
lots of **rattles (pl)**

reach (v)
reaches, reaching, reached
1. to get to a place
2. to stretch to get something

read (v)
reads; reading; read (say red) to understand the meaning of printed words

ready
to be prepared for something

real
something true and not imaginary

really
truly

reason (n)
why something happens or why you do something
lots of **reasons (pl)**

recipe (n)
instructions for cooking food
lots of **recipes (pl)**

record (n)
1. information that is kept
2. something done better than anyone else: **World Record**, something done better than anyone else in the world.
3. a musical disc
lots of **records (pl)**

recorder (n)
a musical instrument you blow into to make a sound
lots of **recorders (pl)**

referee (n)
a person who makes sure games are fair
lots of **referees (pl)**

reflection (n)
what you see when you look into the mirror
lots of **reflections (pl)**

refuse (v)
refuses; refusing; refused
to say 'no' to something

a
b
c
d
e
f
g
h
i
j
k
l
m
n
o
p
q
r
s
t
u
v
w
x
y
z

register

register (n)
a list of names
lots of **registers (pl)**

regular
evenly spaced, normal; usual

relation (n)
a member of your family;
a relative
lots of **relations (pl)**

religion (n)
the worship of and belief in one
or more gods
lots of **religions (pl)**

remember (v)
**remembers; remembering;
remembered**
to keep in the memory

remind (v)
**reminds; reminding;
reminded**
to help someone to remember

reply (v)
replies; replying; replied
to give an answer

rescue (v)
rescues; rescuing; rescued
to save from harm

rest
1. **(v) rests; resting; rested**
to take a break from activity
2. **(n)** all the others

restaurant (n)
a place where meals are made
and sold
lots of **restaurants (pl)**

return (v)
returns; returning; returned
to come or go back

rhyme (n)
a word ending in the same
sound as another word
lots of **rhymes (pl)**

rhythm (n)
a regular pattern of beats
lots of **rhythms (pl)**

ribbon (n)
a strip of material used for
decoration
lots of **ribbons (pl)**

rice (n)
a food grain
lots of **rice**

rich
having lots of money

ride (v)
rides; riding; rode
to travel on something

right
1. correct
2. **(n)** the side opposite to left
! write !

ring
1. **(n)** something you wear on your finger shaped like a circle
lots of **rings (pl)**

2. **(v) rings; ringing; rang**
the noise a bell makes

ripe
ready to eat

rise (v)
rises; rising; rose
to go up

river (n)
a wide stream of water
lots of **rivers (pl)**

road (n)
a track for wheeled vehicles
lots of **roads (pl)**

rock
1. **(n)** a large stone
2. **(v) rocks; rocking; rocked** to move backwards and forwards

roll
1. **(n)** a small loaf of bread
lots of **rolls (pl)**
2. **(v) rolls; rolling; rolled**
to turn over and over

a
b
c
d
e
f
g
h
i
j
k
l
m
n
o
p
q
r
s
t
u
v
w
x
y
z

a
b
c
d
e
f
g
h
i
j
k
l
m
n
o
p
q
r
s
t
u
v
w
x
y
z

roof (n)
the fixed covering on top of a building
lots of **roofs (pl)**

room (n)
one inside section of a building
lots of **rooms (pl)**

root (n)
the part of a plant that grows under the ground
lots of **roots (pl)**

rope (n)
thick string
lots of **ropes (pl)**

round
shaped like a circle or ball

royal
to do with kings, queens and their families

rubber (n)
1. springy strong material used in car tyres
2. something you use to remove pencil marks

rubbish (n)
things thrown away
lots of **rubbish (pl)**

rude
not polite: having bad manners

rug (n)
a floor mat
lots of **rugs (pl)**

rule (n)
what you must do or how you should behave
lots of **rules (pl)**

ruler (n)
1. someone who is in charge of a country, e.g. a king or queen
2. a measuring stick
lots of **rulers (pl)**

S s

sack (n)
a large bag
lots of **sacks (pl)**

sad
unhappy

saddle (n)
a seat for a rider on a horse or bicycle
lots of **saddles (pl)**

bicycle saddle

riding saddle

safe
in no danger

sale (n)
selling something; selling things for less than usual
lots of **sales (pl)**

same
just like something else

sand (n)
powder made of very small grains of rock found by the sea and in deserts

sandwich (n)
two slices of bread with filling in the middle
lots of **sandwiches (pl)**

sauce (n)
a flavoured liquid served with or on food, e.g. tomato **sauce**

sausage (n)
meat made into a tube
lots of **sausages (pl)**

save (v)
saves; saving; saved
1. to rescue
2. to keep for later use

a
b
c
d
e
f
g
h
i
j
k
l
m
n
o
p
q
r
s
t
u
v
w
x
y
z

scare
scares; scaring; scared
to frighten someone: **scary**

scarf (n)
cloth worn round the head
and/or shoulders
lots of **scarves (pl)**

scent
the way something smells
!sent! lots of **scents (pl)**

school (n)
a place where people go
to learn
lots of **schools (pl)**

science (n)
the study of plants, animals and
materials

scissors (n)
cutting tool with two blades

scooter (n)
a child's toy with wheels, a
board to stand on and handles
to hold; it is moved by pushing
the foot on the ground
lots of **scooters (pl)**

score (n)
the points you get in a game
lots of **scores (pl)**

scratch (v)
**scratches; scratching;
scratched**
to mark with a sharp object

scream (v)
**screams; screaming;
screamed**
a loud high cry

sea (n)
a huge area of salty water

seat (n)
somewhere to sit; **seatbelt**:
a safety strap
many **seats (pl)**

second
1. the place after first
2. **(n)** a short length of time,
there are 60 seconds in a
minute, 60 **seconds (pl)**

secret (n)
something only a few
people know
lots of **secrets (pl)**

seed (n)
the part of a plant that can
grow into a new plant
lots of **seeds (pl)**

sell (v)
sells; selling; sold
to give to someone for money

send (v)
sends; sending; sent
to make something or
someone go somewhere

sense (n)
knowing what's reasonable;
sensible: having good sense

senses (n, pl)
how we see, smell, feel, hear or
taste; we have five of these

sentence (n)
a group of words that
have meaning
lots of **sentences (pl)**

separate
apart from other things; not
together

serious
important; not to be joked about

settee (n)
a soft seat for two or more
people; a sofa
lots of **settees (pl)**

a b c d e f g h i j k l m n o p q r **s** t u v w x y z

a
b
c
d
e
f
g
h
i
j
k
l
m
n
o
p
q
r
s
t
u
v
w
x
y
z

sew (v)
sews; sewing; sewed
to join materials together using a needle and thread

shadow (n)
a dark shape which is made when light falls on something
lots of **shadows (pl)**

shall
used with I or we when talking about something you are going to do

shampoo (n)
soapy liquid for washing hair
lots of **shampoo**

shape (n)
the outline or form of an object
lots of **shapes (pl)**

share (v)
shares; sharing; shared
to divide something up between two or more people

sharp
a pointed end; able to cut or pierce

shed (n)
a hut, often wooden, for storing things
lots of **sheds (pl)**

sheet (n)
1. material for covering a bed
2. a piece of paper
lots of **sheets (pl)**

shelf (n)
a long flat piece of wood or metal attached to the wall to stand objects on
many **shelves (pl)**

shell (n)
the hard covering of an animal or nut
lots of **shells (pl)**

ship (n)
a large floating vehicle to carry people or things on water
lots of **ships (pl)**

shirt (n)
clothing for the upper body
lots of **shirts (pl)**

shiver (v)
shivers; shivering; shivered
to shake when cold

shoe (n)
an item worn on your feet
lots of **shoes (pl)**

shop (n)
a place where things are sold
lots of **shops (pl)**

short
not very long

shorts (n)
trousers ending above the knee

a b c d e f g h i j k l m n o p q r **s** t u v w x y z

shout

shout (v)
shouts; shouting; shouted
to speak very loudly

show
1. **(v) shows; showing; showed**
to let someone look at
2. **(n)** a performance
lots of **performances (pl)**

shower (n)
1. a short fall of rain
2. machine used for washing the body
lots of **showers (pl)**

sick
ill and being unwell

side (n)
one edge or surface of something
lots of **sides (pl)**

sight (n)
the sense of seeing; use of the eye

sign (n)
something which gives information
lots of **signs (pl)**

silence (n)
no noise at all

silver (n)
a valuable metal used for jewellery and coins
lots of **silver**

similar
a lot like something else

simple
easy to do or understand

since
between then and now

sink
1. **(v) sinks; sinking; sank**
to go down under water
2. **(n)** a basin in the kitchen for washing dishes
lots of **sinks (pl)**

skate

1. **(v) skates; skating; skated** to glide along a surface
2. **(n)** footwear with wheels or blades to glide on: **ice skates** and **roller skates**
lots of **skates (pl)**

roller skates

ice skates

skateboard **(n)**

a fun thing made of board to stand on and wheels to skate on
lots of **skateboards (pl)**

skeleton **(n)**

the bones in a body
lots of **skeletons (pl)**

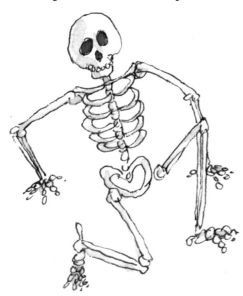

ski

long object fastened to the feet for travel on snow or water;
skiing

skin **(n)**

the natural outer covering of a body

skip **(v)**

skips; skipping; skipped
to move with quick steps and jumps

skirt **(n)**

female clothing that hangs from the waist
lots of **skirts (pl)**

sky **(n)**

air above us where we see the sun, moon and stars

sleep **(v)**

sleeps; sleeping; slept
to rest at night: the time when you dream

a
b
c
d
e
f
g
h
i
j
k
l
m
n
o
p
q
r
s
t
u
v
w
x
y
z

a
b
c
d
e
f
g
h
i
j
k
l
m
n
o
p
q
r
s
t
u
v
w
x
y
z

sleeve (n)
the part of clothing that covers
the arm
lots of **sleeves (pl)**

slice (n)
a thin piece cut from
something
lots of **slices (pl)**

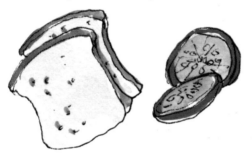

slide
1. **(v) slides; sliding; slid**
to go smoothly over a surface
2. **(n)** apparatus in the park for
moving quickly down
lots of **slides (pl)**

slip (v)
slips; slipping; slipped
to fall by sliding

slow
to take a long time to move,
not quick

small
of little size, not big

smell (n)
the scent given off by
something, e.g. this fish has an
awful smell
lots of **smells (pl)**

smile (n)
how your mouth looks when
you are pleased or happy
lots of **smiles (pl)**

sneeze (v)
sneezes; sneezing; sneezed
air coming fast from your nose

sniff (v)
sniffs; sniffing; sniffed
to draw air into the nose quickly

snow (n)
water frozen into flat flakes
that falls from clouds when it
is very cold
lots of **snow (pl)**

soap (n)
used for washing and cleaning

sock (n)
a soft covering for the foot
a pair of **socks (pl)**

sofa (n)
a soft seat for two or more
people: a settee
lots of **sofas (pl)**

soft
not hard or stiff

soil (n)
the top covering of the ground

some
a small amount

song (n)
a piece of music with words
lots of **songs (pl)**

soon
in a short time

sore
painful

sorry
to feel bad about something
you have done

sound (n)
something you can hear
lots of **sounds (pl)**

soup (n)
a liquid food
lots of **soup (pl)**

space (n)
1. a gap between objects
2. the area outside Earth's air

spade (n)
a tool used for digging
lots of **spades (pl)**

spaghetti (n)
a food: long thin pasta
lots of **spaghetti (pl)**

a
b
c
d
e
f
g
h
i
j
k
l
m
n
o
p
q
r
s
t
u
v
w
x
y
z

spare

spare
an extra one

speak (v)
speaks; speaking; spoke
to use the voice to talk

speed (n)
how fast something moves

spell (v)
spells; spelling; spelt
use letters in order to make
a word

spend (v)
spends; spending; spent
use money to buy things, or use
time doing something

spider (n)
an eight-legged creature which
makes webs
lots of **spiders (pl)**

splash (v)
**splashes; splashing;
splashed**
make liquid move noisily; the
sound it makes

splinter (n)
a very small pointed piece of
wood or glass
lots of **splinters (pl)**

sponge (n)
a material with holes that soaks
up liquid quickly
lots of **sponges (pl)**

spoon (n)
something with a round end
and a handle used for eating
food
lots of **spoons (pl)**

sport (n)
games or activities done for
pleasure

spot
1. **(v) spots; spotting; spotted** to see something
2. **(n)** a small mark on something; a pimple
lots of **spots (pl)**

squash
1. **(v) squashes; squashing; squashed** to squeeze flat
2. **(n)** a fruit drink

squeeze (v)
squeezes; squeezing; squeezed
to press from each side

stairs (n)
steps between floors in a building

stamp
1. **(v) stamps; stamping; stamped** put the foot down quickly and hard
2. **(n)** a printing tool
3. **(n)** a sticky piece of paper stuck on an envelope to show payment for posting
lots of **stamps (pl)**

stand (v)
stands; standing; stood
to stay upright supported on legs

star (n)
1. one of many bright lights in the night sky
2. a famous person
lots of **stars (pl)**

stare (v)
stares; staring; stared
to look at something for a long time

a b c d e f g h i j k l m n o p q r **s** t u v w x y z

a
b
c
d
e
f
g
h
i
j
k
l
m
n
o
p
q
r
s
t
u
v
w
x
y
z

start (v)
starts; starting; started
to begin

stay (v)
stays; staying; stayed
to remain in a place

steal (v)
steals; stealing; stole
to take something which isn't
yours

steam (n)
the cloudy gas from boiling
water
lots of **steam (pl)**

steer (v)
steers; steering; steered
to guide something, usually
a vehicle

stem (n)
the part of a flower that holds
the leaves and flower
lots of **stems (pl)**

step
1. **(n)** a stair, lots of **steps (pl)**
2. **(v) steps, stepping,**
stepped to put down a foot

stick
1. **(n)** a long thin piece of wood
lots of **sticks (pl)**
2. **(v) sticks; sticking; stuck**
to join things together with glue

still
not moving

sting (v)
stings; stinging; stung
a sharp pain, from an insect
or plant

stir (v)
stirs; stirring; stirred
move round to mix together

stone (n)
1. a piece of rock
2. a hard seed in some fruit
lots of **stones (pl)**

stool (n)
a seat with no back
lots of **stools (pl)**

stop (v)
stops; stopping; stopped
finish moving or doing
something

storm (n)
very bad weather often with
wind, rain, thunder and
lightning
lots of **storms (pl)**

story (n)
a tale about something
lots of **stories (pl)**

straight
not bent or curved

strange
odd or unusual

stranger (n)
a person you do not know
lots of **strangers (pl)**

strap (n)
a strong strip of material made
for holding things
lots of **straps (pl)**

stream (n)
a small natural flow of water
lots of **streams (pl)**

street (n)
a road with houses on it
many **streets (pl)**

strength (n)
how strong something is

stretch (v)
**stretches; stretching;
stretched**
to make something bigger by
pulling

string (n)
a strong thread used to tie
things

stripe (n)
a band of colour
lots of **stripes (pl)**

stroke (v)
strokes; stroking; stroked
to smooth with the hand

a
b
c
d
e
f
g
h
i
j
k
l
m
n
o
p
q
r
s
t
u
v
w
x
y
z

strong

not easily broken; powerful

student (n)

a person learning at a school or college; someone who studies
lots of **students (pl)**

sudden

happening without warning unexpectedly; **suddenly**

sugar (n)

substance used to make food sweet
lots of **sugar**

sum (n)

what is made when you add numbers together
lots of **sums (pl)**

sun (n)

the round circle in the sky that gives light and heat; it is a giant star

supermarket (n)

a large shop where you buy food and other things
lots of **supermarkets (pl)**

sure

in no doubt

surname (n)

your family name
lots of **surnames (pl)**

surprise (n)

something unexpected
lots of **surprises (pl)**

swallow (v)

swallow; swallowing; swallowed
to move food or drink from the throat into the stomach

sweat (n)

liquid which comes from the skin when you get hot
lots of **sweat**

sweet

food that tastes like sugar

Tt

table (n)
furniture on legs with a flat top
lots of **tables (pl)**

tail (n)
the long, thin part at the back
of most animals **!tale!**
lots of **tails (pl)**

tale (n)
a story **!tail!**
lots of **tales (pl)**

talk (v)
talks; talking; talked
to use the voice to speak

tall
quite high; not short

tap (n)
the metal part of a sink that
controls the flow of water
lots of **taps (pl)**

tape (n)
a strip of material, sticky plastic
or paper

tape recorder (n)
a machine able to record sounds
on tape and play them back
lots of **tape recorders**

taste
1. **(v) tastes; tasting; tasted**
to try food or drink in the
mouth
2. **(n)** the sense which tells us
which food is which

tea (n)
a drink made from tea leaves

a b c d e f g h i j k l m n o p q r s t u v w x y z

teach

a b c d e f g h i j k l m n o p q r s **t** u v w x y z

teach (v)
teaches; teaching; taught
to train or give lessons

team (n)
a group of people working or
playing a game together
many **teams (pl)**

tease (v)
teases; teasing; teased
to make fun of

teeth (n, pl)
(see tooth)

telephone (n)
(see **phone**)
lots of **telephones (pl)**

television (n)
a machine on which you can
watch programmes and films
lots of **televisions (pl)**

tell (v)
tells; telling; told
to say something to someone

temperature (n)
how hot or cold something is

tent (n)
a movable shelter made of
material
lots of **tents (pl)**

terrible
very bad or frightening

test
1. **(v) tests; testing; tested**
to try something out
2. **(n)** activities to find out what
people know or can do
lots of **tests (pl)**

88

thank (v)
thanks; thanking; thanked
to say you are grateful for
something

that
the one described or shown

their
belonging to them **!there!**

thermometer (n)
instrument used to measure
temperature
lots of **thermometers (pl)**

they
the ones being talked about

thick
wide: not thin

thief (n)
a person who steals
lots of **thieves (pl)**

thin
not fat or wide

thing (n)
any object that can be touched
or seen
lots of **things (pl)**

think (v)
thinks; thinking; thought
to use your mind

thirst (n)
feeling a need for a drink: **thirsty**

thought (n)
an idea in the mind (see **think**)
lots of **thoughts (pl)**

through
across, between or in the middle
of, e.g. this road goes **through**
the centre of town

throw (v)
throws; throwing; threw
to send anything through the air
using your arm

thumb (n)
you have four fingers and one
of these on each hand
lots of **thumbs (pl)**

a
b
c
d
e
f
g
h
i
j
k
l
m
n
o
p
q
r
s
t
u
v
w
x
y
z

a
b
c
d
e
f
g
h
i
j
k
l
m
n
o
p
q
r
s
t
u
v
w
x
y
z

thunder (n)
the noisy part of a storm
lots of **thunder**

ticket (n)
a piece of paper showing you
have paid for a journey or event
like the theatre or cinema
lots of **tickets (pl)**

tickle (n)
a feeling on the skin caused by
a light touch; it makes you laugh

tidy
not in a mess; arranged neatly

tie
1. **(v) ties; tying; tied**
to fasten with string or
rope
2. **(n)** material that goes round
your neck
lots of **ties (pl)**

tight
fitting closely; not loose

till (n)
a machine in a shop which adds
and stores money
lots of **tills (pl)**

time (n)
the passing of hours, days,
weeks, months, years

tin (n)
a silver-coloured metal often
used to make cans

tired
in need of sleep

tissue (n)
soft paper, often used to blow
the nose
lots of **tissues (pl)**

title (n)
the name of a book or film
lots of **titles (pl)**

toast
1. **(n)** bread put in front of heat
until it is brown
lots of **toast (pl)**
2. **(v) toasts; toasting;
toasted** the way bread is
browned

today (n)
this day now

together
in the same place

toilet (n)
you use this to get rid of waste body matter
lots of **toilets (pl)**

tomorrow (n)
the day after this one

tongue (n)
a thing in the mouth to help you to eat and speak
lots of **tongues (pl)**

tonight (n)
the night of this day; when it is dark and the moon and stars come out

tool (n)
an instrument for a particular job
lots of **tools (pl)**

tooth (n)
one of the hard white bits inside your mouth used for biting and chewing food
lots of **teeth (pl)**

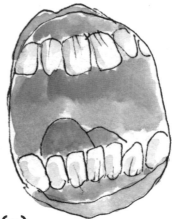

top (n)
1. the highest point
2. a child's spinning toy
lots of **tops (pl)**

touch (v)
touches; touching; touched
to feel with a part of the body

towel (n)
material used to dry wet things
lots of **towels (pl)**

town (n)
an area made up of a large group of buildings where people live and work, bigger than a village
lots of **towns (pl)**

a
b
c
d
e
f
g
h
i
j
k
l
m
n
o
p
q
r
s
t
u
v
w
x
y
z

toy (n)
an object for children to play with
lots of **toys (pl)**

traffic (n)
all the vehicles, like cars and lorries, moving on a road
lots of **traffic**

trainer (n)
one of a pair of shoes worn for playing sport
a pair of **trainers (pl)**

tree (n)
a tall plant with a trunk made of wood, branches, twigs and leaves
lots of **trees (pl)**

trouble (n)
a difficulty or problem

trousers (n)
clothing for the legs

true
real; not a lie; the truth

try (v)
tries; trying; tried
to have a go at something

T-shirt (n)
lots of **T-shirts (pl)**

tube (n)
a hollow round pipe
lots of **tubes (pl)**

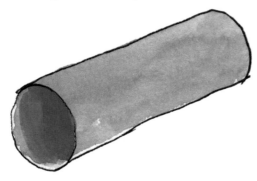

tumble (v)
tumbles; tumbling; tumbled
to fall over

tune (n)
a number of musical notes
put together to make music, like
a song
lots of **tunes (pl)**

turn (v)
turns; turning; turned
to move round and round

twice
two times

twig (n)
a thin stem on the branch of
a tree
lots of **twigs (pl)**

twin (n)
one of two children born at the
same time: they sometimes
look alike
a pair of **twins (pl)**

twist (v)
twists; twisting; twisted
to turn part of something

tyre (n)
a thick rubber tube used on a
wheel
lots of **tyres (pl)**

a b c d e f g h i j k l m n o p q r s **t** u v w x y z

a
b
c
d
e
f
g
h
i
j
k
l
m
n
o
p
q
r
s
t
u
v
w
x
y
z

Uu

ugly
not nice to look at

umbrella (n)
an object to keep the rain off
lots of **umbrellas (pl)**

un
sometimes the letters **un** are put in front of a word to make it the opposite of a word; for example **unhappy** means not happy

understand (v)
understands; understanding; understood
to know the meaning of

underwear (n)
clothes worn under other clothes, e.g. pants or knickers
lot of underwear

undo (v)
undoes; undoing; undone
put something as it was before

undress (v)
undresses; undressing; undressed
to take your clothes off

uniform (n)
clothes worn to show you belong to a group or team
lots of **uniforms (pl)**

until
up to that time

upset
not happy about something; sad or cross

upside down
the wrong way up

upstairs
on an upper floor of a building

use (v)
uses; using; used
to do something with an object, e.g. I **use** a toothbrush each day

usual
normal

Vv

vacuum cleaner (n)
a machine that works by
sucking up dirt
lots of **vacuum cleaners (pl)**

value (n)
what a thing is worth

vanish (v)
**vanishes; vanishing;
vanished**
to go out of sight; to disappear

vase (n)
a container for holding cut
flowers
lots of **vases (pl)**

vegetable (n)
lots of **vegetables (pl)**
see page 121

vegetarian
the word to describe a person
who does not eat meat

vehicle (n)
a type of machine for transport
such as cars, lorries, boats,
aeroplanes
lots of **vehicles (pl)**

very
a lot, a large amount

vest (n)
underwear for the upper body
lots of **vests (pl)**

a
b
c
d
e
f
g
h
i
j
k
l
m
n
o
p
q
r
s
t
u
v
w
x
y
z

vet (n)
an animal doctor
lots of **vets (pl)**

video (n)
a film for showing on your TV
using a video recorder
lots of **videos (pl)**

view (n)
what you can see
lots of **views (pl)**

village (n)
a collection of buildings where
people live, smaller than
a town
lots of **villages (pl)**

vinegar (n)
an acid liquid used to flavour
food
lots of **vinegar (pl)**

visit (v)
visits; visiting; visited
to go to see someone or
something

voice (n)
the sounds we make when we
speak or sing
many **voices (pl)**

volcano (n)
a place where hot rocks and gas
are blown out of the earth
lots of **volcanoes (pl)**

vowel (n)
the letters a, e, i, o and u and
their sounds
five **vowels (pl)**

Ww

wage, wages (n)
the money you are paid for
doing a job

wait (v)
waits; waiting; waited
to stay somewhere until
something happens

wake up (v)
wakes; waking; woke
to stop sleeping

walk (v)
walks; walking; walked
to move by putting one foot in
front of the other

wall (n)
lots of **walls (pl)**

want (v)
want; wanting; wanted
to have a desire or wish for
something

wardrobe (n)
furniture to hang your clothes in
lots of **wardrobes (pl)**

warm
a little bit hot; not cold

wash (v)
wash; washing; washed
to make clean

washing machine (n)
a machine for washing clothes
lots of **washing machines
(pl)**

a
b
c
d
e
f
g
h
i
j
k
l
m
n
o
p
q
r
s
t
u
v
w
x
y
z

a
b
c
d
e
f
g
h
i
j
k
l
m
n
o
p
q
r
s
t
u
v
w
x
y
z

waste (n)
things thrown away; rubbish
lots of **waste**

watch
1. **(v) watches; watching; watched**
look at something for a while
2. **(n)** a small clock to wear on your wrist or on a chain
lots of **watches (pl)**

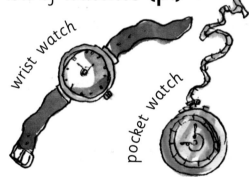
wrist watch
pocket watch

water (n)
a clear liquid which falls as rain from clouds
lots of **water (pl)**

wave
1. **(v) waves; waving; waved** move a hand from side to side in the air
2. **(n)** the moving of the sea
many **waves (pl)**

weak
not strong; easily broken
!week!

wear (v)
wears; wearing; wore
to carry on the body

weather (n)
rain, sun, wind, snow and hail

web (n)
1. a spider's home
lots of **webs (pl)**
2. short for website, see page 127

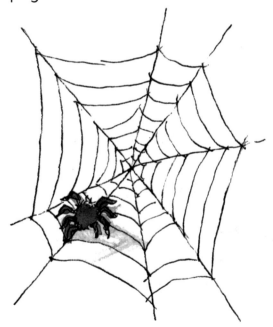

week (n)
seven days and nights **!weak!**
lots of **weeks (pl)**

weight (n)
how heavy something is

well
1. not ill
2. **(n)** a water or oil source below ground
lots of **wells (pl)**

wet
covered in liquid; not dry

wheel **(n)**
round object used to help vehicles such as cars, lorries and bicycles move along
lots of **wheels (pl)**

 bicycle wheel

 car wheel

while
all the time that

whisper **(v)**
whispers; whispering; whispered
to speak very quietly

whistle
1. **(v) whistles; whistling; whistled** to make a sound by blowing through the lips
2. **(n)** an instrument to make this sound, lots of **whistles (pl)**

whole
complete; all of something

wide
a long way from side to side

wild
not tamed

will
something to be done in the future, e.g. He **will** go tomorrow

win **(v)**
wins; winning; won
to come first in a race or competition

a b c d e f g h i j k l m n o p q r s t u v **w** x y z

wind (n)
a type of weather condition where air moves quickly

window (n)
an opening in a wall for light and air
lots of **windows (pl)**

wing (n)
the parts of a bird or plane which help it to fly
lots of **wings (pl)**

aeroplane wings

bird wings

wire (n)
very thin metal thread

wish (v)
wishes; wishing; wished
to want something

witch (n)
a woman in stories who can do magic
lots of **witches (pl)**

without
to not have something

wizard (n)
a man in stories who can do magic
lots of **wizards (pl)**

woman (n)
a grown-up female
lots of **women (pl)**

wonder (v)
wonders; wondering; wondered
to wish to know

wood (n)
1. a material that comes from trees; **wooden**
2. a place where lots of trees grow, e.g. a forest

wool (n)
the soft hair of some animals, especially sheep
lots of **wool (pl)**

word (n)
letters that mean something when put together in order;
lots of **words (pl)**

work (v)
works; working; worked
to do an activity for a purpose; a job

world (n)
everything around us: the Earth and its people

worm (n)
a small thin creature with no bones or legs
lots of **worms (pl)**

worry (v)
worries; worrying; worried
to feel concern for something

worse
not as good as something else: bad

wriggle (v)
wriggles; wriggling; wriggled
to twist from side to side

write (v)
writes; writing; wrote
make letters or words **!right!**

wrong
not right; incorrect

a
b
c
d
e
f
g
h
i
j
k
l
m
n
o
p
q
r
s
t
u
v
w
x
y
z

Xx

x-ray (n)
a photograph of the inside of
something
lots of **x-rays (pl)**

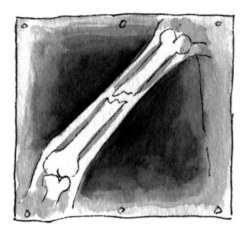

xylophone (n)
a musical instrument made of
wooden bars
lots of **xylophones (pl)**

a b c d e f g h i j k l m n o p q r s t u v w **x** y z

Yy

yacht (n)
a type of sailing boat
lots of **yachts**

yawn (v)
yawns; yawning; yawned
a deep breath you take with an
open mouth when you are tired

year (n)
12 months of time
many **years (pl)**

yesterday (n)
the day before this day

yoghurt (n)
a thick pudding made from milk,
often with fruit
lots of **yoghurt**

yolk (n)
the yellow part of an egg
lots of **yolks (pl)**

you
not me but the other person

young
not very old

your
belonging to you

yo-yo (n)
a toy on a string which goes up
and down
lots of **yo-yos (pl)**

a
b
c
d
e
f
g
h
i
j
k
l
m
n
o
p
q
r
s
t
u
v
w
x
y
z

a
b
c
d
e
f
g
h
i
j
k
l
m
n
o
p
q
r
s
t
u
v
w
x
y
z

Z z

zebra (n)
an animal with black and white stripes
lots of **zebras (pl)**

zebra crossing (n)
a place for crossing the road marked with black and white stripes
lots of **zebra crossings (pl)**

zero (n)
the figure 0; nought; nothing; nil

zigzag (v)
a pattern of lines that looks like the letter Z
lots of **zigzags (pl)**

zip (n)
a type of fastening, especially for trousers and jackets
lots of **zips (pl)**

zoo (n)
a collection of wild animals in a place where people can go and see them
lots of **zoos (pl)**

Months

January	May	September
February	June	October
March	July	November
April	August	December

Days of the week

Sunday	Wednesday	Saturday
Monday	Thursday	
Tuesday	Friday	

Compass points

North

West East

South

Seasons of the year

spring

summer

autumn

winter

Numbers

Cardinal numbers

0 nought/zero	**11** eleven	**40** forty
1 one	**12** twelve	**50** fifty
2 two	**13** thirteen	**60** sixty
3 three	**14** fourteen	**70** seventy
4 four	**15** fifteen	**80** eighty
5 five	**16** sixteen	**90** ninety
6 six	**17** seventeen	**100** one hundred
7 seven	**18** eighteen	**500** five hundred
8 eight	**19** nineteen	**1000** one thousand
9 nine	**20** twenty	**1,000,000** one million
10 ten	**30** thirty	

Ordinal numbers

1st first	**6th** sixth	**11th** eleventh
2nd second	**7th** seventh	**12th** twelfth
3rd third	**8th** eighth	**20th** twentieth
4th fourth	**9th** ninth	**100th** hundredth
5th fifth	**10th** tenth	**1000th** thousandth

Measurements

Length

mm millimetres   10mm = 1cm

cm centimetres 100cm = 1m

m metres   1000m = 1km

km kilometres

Weight

mg milligrams 1000mg = 1g

g grams   1000mg = 1kg

kg kilograms

Capacity

ml millilitres   10ml = 1cl

cl centilitres   100cl = 1l

l litres

Shapes

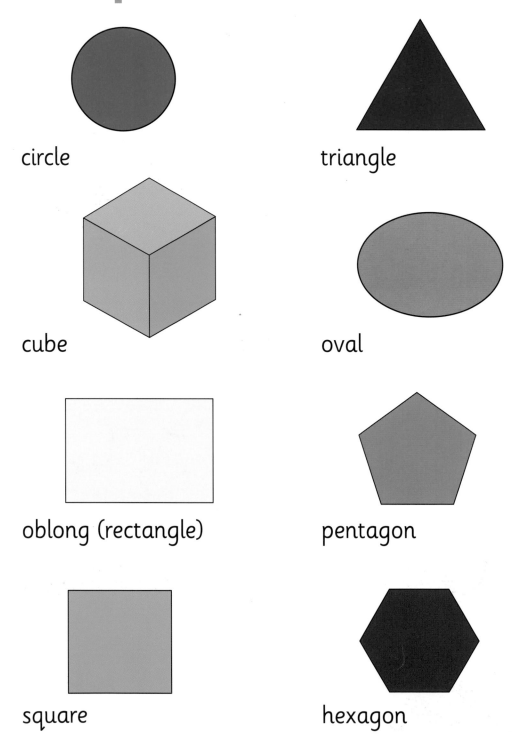

circle

triangle

cube

oval

oblong (rectangle)

pentagon

square

hexagon

Colours

red

brown

orange

black

yellow

white

green

pink

blue

grey

purple

Opposites

above   below

awake   asleep

before   after

top   bottom

begin   end

open   closed

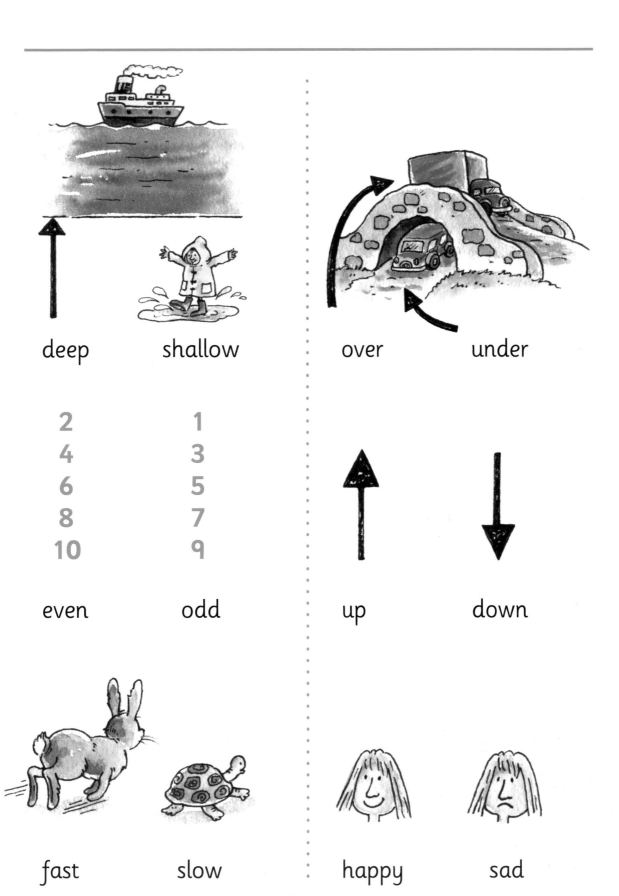

deep   shallow   over   under

2	1
4	3
6	5
8	7
10	9

even   odd   up   down

fast   slow   happy   sad

Animals

alligator

badger

bear

cat

cow

crocodile

dog

dolphin

donkey

duck

elephant

fox

114

gorilla   hedgehog   hen   horse

kangaroo   lion   monkey   penguin

pig   rabbit   shark   sheep

snake   tiger   whale   zebra

The body

External

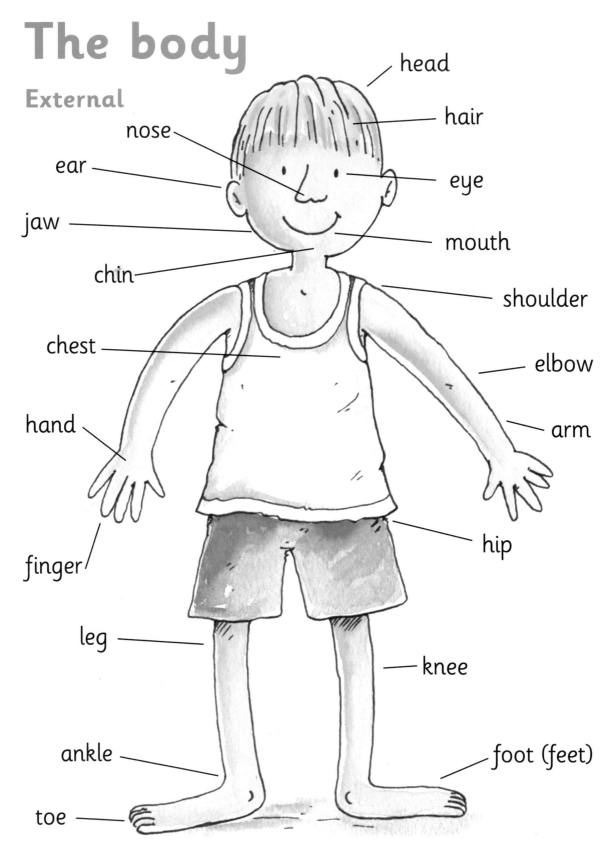

head

hair

eye

mouth

shoulder

elbow

arm

hip

knee

foot (feet)

nose

ear

jaw

chin

chest

hand

finger

leg

ankle

toe

Internal

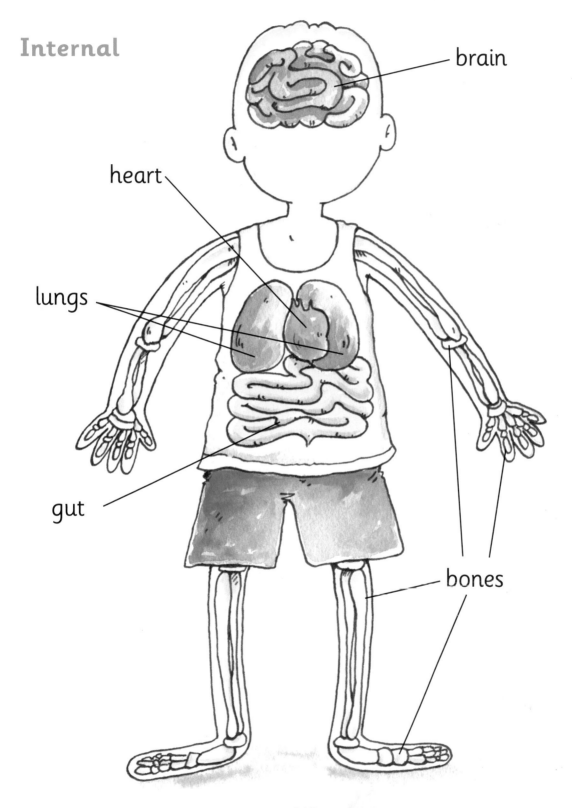

brain

heart

lungs

gut

bones

Family

grandmother
grandma

mum
mother

sister

grandfather
grandpa

dad
father

brother

Other relatives

aunt   uncle   niece   nephew   cousin

Vehicles

aeroplane

ambulance

bus

car

fire engine

lorry

motorbike

tractor

van

Fruit

apple

banana

melon

orange

nut

peach

pear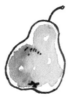

pineapple

raspberry

strawberry

tomato

lemon

Vegetables

bean

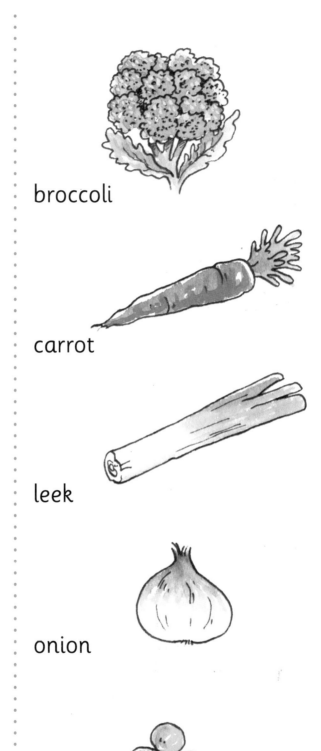

broccoli

cabbage

carrot

cauliflower

leek

lettuce

onion

potato

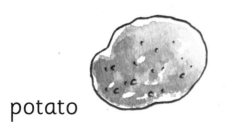

pea

Short useful words

a	and	each	but	for
he	him	his	in	into
is	it	just	let	me
my	mine	of	off	on
onto	or	put	she	her
hers	so	the	then	there
this	to	too	us	was
we	with			

Question words

how	what	when	where
which	who	whose	why

Parts of speech

Nouns
the name of something

tree   house   car   school

Proper nouns
names of people or places begin with a capital letter

Andrew   Lauren   London   Paris

Adjectives
describe a thing

beautiful   nasty   lucky   difficult

Adverbs
describe an action

quickly   well   strongly   nicely

Prepositions
describe positions or directions

at   by   for   with   between

in   on   to   underneath

Verbs

doing words

be   am, are, is, being, been, was, were

buy   buys, buying, bought

carry   carries, carrying, carried

come   comes, coming, came

do   does, doing, did, done

get   gets, getting, got

give   gives, giving, gave, given

go   goes, going, went, gone

have   has, having, had

run   runs, running, ran

say   says, saying, said

see   sees, seeing, saw, seen

sing   sings, singing, sang, sung

sit   sits, sitting, sat

swim   swims, swimming, swam, swum

take   takes, taking, took, taken

Science and technology

disc
a round piece of plastic for storing music

disk
like a disk but for storing electronic information

electricity
a type of power, from batteries or along wires

electronic
a machine which uses electricity

fax
a copy of anything on a piece of paper sent electronically; **(facsimile) fax machine**

ozone layer
gas in the sky which protects the Earth from the sun's rays

robot
a machine that can do some human work

rocket
a spacecraft powered by burning gas

satellite dish
a receiver for television from a satellite going round the Earth

science
the study of natural laws

technology
the use of science

applications
a program that lets you use your computer for a particular kind of job, like writing, drawing or doing sums

clipboard
the place where your computer stores something that you move or copy, like a picture or some writing

database
a store for detailed information (permanent)

delete
a key that gets rid of mistakes and old files

digital
systems using electronic codes, e.g. digital camera

document
a piece of work (file) created using an application

edit
to correct or alter a piece of work

file
a collection of information stored in a computer

folder
for storing several files

font
the different styles of letters that you can choose for your documents

graphics
programs for drawing or illustrating

icon
a picture representing an application or file

menu
a list of applications, programs or options that you can use

network
several computers linked together

program
the instructions that control how a computer works

spreadsheet
an application that helps you to work with numbers

toolbar
a row of control buttons on the screen

window
a box-shaped area on the screen which you can open up to work on something inside

word processing
using a computer application to write something

internet
a system which allows computers everywhere to be connected

browsing
looking for sources of information

download
to move information from the internet onto your computer

email
sending messages to other computers electronically

surfing
looking at several websites

web
a system which allows people everywhere to share information on their computers

website
a place on the internet with information on a particular subject

Information technology

Hardware

computer (PC)

desktop

monitor

printer

joystick

keyboard

mouse

Software

CD ROM   (floppy) disk   DVD